William Jones Hoppin

Proceedings of the Century Association

in Honor of the Memory of Brig.-Gen. James S. Wadsworth and Colonel

Peter A. Porter

William Jones Hoppin

Proceedings of the Century Association
in Honor of the Memory of Brig.-Gen. James S. Wadsworth and Colonel Peter A. Porter

ISBN/EAN: 9783337092610

Printed in Europe, USA, Canada, Australia, Japan

Cover: Foto ©ninafisch / pixelio.de

More available books at **www.hansebooks.com**

PROCEEDINGS

OF THE

CENTURY ASSOCIATION

IN HONOR OF THE MEMORY OF

BRIG.-GEN. JAMES S. WADSWORTH

AND

COLONEL PETER A. PORTER;

WITH

THE EULOGIES

READ BY

WILLIAM J. HOPPIN AND FREDERIC S. COZZENS.

DECEMBER 3, 1864.

NEW YORK:
D. VAN NOSTRAND, 192 BROADWAY.
M DCCC LXV.

PROCEEDINGS

OF

"THE CENTURY."

DURING the summer of 1864, the Century Association appointed committees to report resolutions at the November meeting, expressive of the respect cherished by the Association for the memory of the late General Wadsworth and Colonel Porter.

The first of these committees consisted of the following gentlemen :

GEORGE BANCROFT,	JOHN JAY,
CHARLES P. DALY,	JAMES W. BEEKMAN,
FRANCIS LIEBER,	JOHN J. ASTOR,
WILLIAM M. EVARTS,	BENJAMIN R. WINTHROP,
DANIEL HUNTINGTON,	GEORGE T. STRONG, and
WILLIAM C. BRYANT,	WILLIAM J. HOPPIN.

This committee afterwards appointed Mr. Evarts to prepare the resolutions, and Mr. Hoppin to read an account of the life and services of General Wadsworth.

The second committee included the following gentlemen:

JOHN VAN BUREN,   DANIEL HUNTINGTON,
LEWIS RUTHERFORD,   JOSEPH H. CHOATE,
CHARLES H. OGDEN,   WILLIAM E. CURTIS, and
              A. RODNEY MACDONOUGH.

Mr. Macdonough was chosen by them to prepare the resolutions, and Mr. Frederic S. Cozzens to read a paper upon the public life and character of Colonel Porter.

The celebration of Mr. Bryant's birthday having been appointed for the November meeting, it was decided to postpone the reports of these committees until the first Saturday in December.

On that evening, after the regular business of the Association had been transacted, Mr. Hoppin read a Eulogy upon General Wadsworth; upon the conclusion of which Mr. Evarts offered the following resolutions, which were unanimously adopted, and ordered to be entered on the minutes:

Resolved, That in the death of General Wadsworth society has lost one of its brightest ornaments, the State of New York one of its most eminent citizens, and the country one of its greatest patriots and bravest soldiers.

Resolved, That the most generous impulses of public spirit and of ardent patriotism inspired the prompt and persistent resolution with which General Wadsworth forsook every attraction and enjoyment of private life with which his wealth and his family, his talents and his education surrounded him, and from the first outbreak of the Rebellion devoted himself, his means, his influence, his labors, to the support of his Government, and at last laid down his life a sacrifice to the welfare, the safety, the honor of his country.

Resolved, That the manner of his death, in the front of battle, at the head of his command, in the severest conflict of the war, was an illustrious close of a noble life; and notwithstanding the great public loss and the manifold private griefs which attend his death, we must yet pronounce a life thus lived, a life thus closed, complete, heroic, fortunate.

Resolved, That we beg to offer a sincere and respectful sympathy, in their nearer sorrow and deeper affliction, to the family of General Wadsworth, and that we earnestly ask the Government that it will honor his memory by permitting one of the forts of our harbor to bear and commemorate his heroic name.

Mr. Frederic S. Cozzens then read a Eulogy upon the life and services of Colonel Peter A. Porter; after which, Mr. Macdonough, from the committee charged with that duty, presented the following resolutions, which were also adopted unanimously, and ordered to be entered upon the minutes of the Association:

Resolved, That "The Century" deplores, with deep and lasting grief, the death upon the battle-field of their late loved and honored associate, Colonel Peter A. Porter.

Resolved, That we search the annals of this war in vain for a kinder heart, a brighter wit, a purer soul, inspiring a life of culture more finished and purposes more noble, and welcoming a more triumphant martyrdom of all-sacrificing patriotism.

Resolved, That the character of Colonel Porter—tender and steadfast as he was in all home and friendly relations—faithful and intelligent in devotion to the public civil service—modest, humane, and gallant in the career of arms—crowning the graces and accomplishments of the scholar's life with the truest glories of the soldier's, and the genuine faith and practice of the Christian's, burnishes the bright name which he inherited, and stamps it high on the Golden Book of Americans made noble by worth and valor.

Resolved, That the personal sorrow with which "The Century" laments the loss of one endeared to them by so many years of genial companionship, is deepened by the sense that in him the Nation has lost a man of a type it can ill spare; and that the years so rich in promise would have borne, had they matured, ripe fruits of wisdom in council and of courage and resource in action, priceless to his country in that new era, for the dawn of which he gave his hopes, his labors, and his life.

Afterwards, on motion of Mr. John H. Gourlie, it was

Resolved, That "The Century" presents its acknowledgments to Mr. Hoppin and to Mr. Cozzens, for the feeling and elegant manner in which they have prepared the memorials of its esteem for its late associates; that the Eulogies just delivered be printed under the direction of the Board of Management, together with the Resolutions, the expense of printing to be defrayed by subscription, and that the two Committees be discharged, with thanks.

On motion of Dr. Lieber, it was

Resolved, That the committee of which Mr. Evarts is chairman communicate with the War Department with reference to naming a fort in our harbor after General Wadsworth.

MR. HOPPIN'S

EULOGY

ON

GENERAL WADSWORTH.

I HAVE been honored by my associates upon the Committee of Arrangements by a request to write an account of the life and services of our friend and fellow-member, the late General Wadsworth. It would have been better, perhaps, if the performance of this duty had been intrusted to some one who enjoyed more intimate personal relations with him than I did, and who might have enlivened his memorial with anecdotes and recollections which a confidential friendship alone could supply. But it is, after all, with the main facts of Wadsworth's life that we are chiefly concerned, and if I can recite these in such a way as to arouse in your hearts the respect and admiration which they have excited in my own, I shall feel that I am not entirely unworthy of the position to which I have been assigned. It will be enough for me to show, in the simplest words, his high idea of patriotic duty, his unfaltering devotion to it, and the extraordinary sacrifices he made in its pursuit.

2

James Samuel Wadsworth was born at Geneseo on the 30th day of October, 1807. He was the eldest son of James Wadsworth, who had emigrated from Durham, in Connecticut, and whose family was among the most ancient and respectable in that State. It is said that one of his ancestors was that sturdy Puritan, Joseph Wadsworth, the Captain of the train-bands who concealed the precious Charter which Charles II. had given to the Colony, in the famous oak at Hartford, in defiance of the authority of the tyrant Andross ; and who, afterwards, when another intruding Governor, Colonel Fletcher, of New York, attempted to exercise illegal rule over the Connecticut Militia, caused his drums to beat and drown the reading of the Royal Commission, saying to Fletcher, "If I am interrupted, I will make the daylight shine through your body."

James Wadsworth, of Durham, and his brother William, the father and uncle of our friend, made their way to the banks of the Genesee in the year 1790, when that whole region was a rude wilderness, from which the Indians had scarcely been expelled. They opened their path, in some places, by their own axes, and established themselves at a point called "Big Tree," which is now the village of Geneseo. They were the agents of many of the proprietors, whose lands they cleared and brought into market ; and they also, in process of time, became

themselves the most extensive and wealthy landholders
of that neighborhood. Mr. Lewis F. Allen, to whose excellent Memorial of General Wadsworth I am indebted for
some of the information contained in this paper, intimates
that they owed this success to the happy union of their
own personal qualities. William, who had a more stout
and hardy nature than his brother, carried on all the out-
of-door operations, while James, who had received an
excellent education at the East, and acquired habits of
system and order, managed the finances, entertained the
guests, and, by his sound judgment and fine taste, contributed not only to the material prosperity, but to the
picturesque beauty of that famous valley. He had been
graduated at Yale College, and he took into the wild
country to which he emigrated a love for letters and
refined social intercourse which made it blossom early
with the sweet flowers of mental and moral culture.
After the population had sufficiently increased, he caused
tracts upon the subject of popular education to be printed
and circulated at his own expense ; he offered premiums
to the towns which should first establish school libraries ;
he procured the passage of the school library law in 1808 ;
he suggested the establishment of Normal Schools in
1811 ; he founded and endowed a library and system of
lectures at Geneseo ; and he provided that in all his sales
a tract of one hundred and twenty-five acres in every

township should be reserved for a church, and as much more for a school. When he died, in 1844, his gifts to the cause of Education alone had exceeded the sum of ninety thousand dollars.

His wife, and the mother of our friend, a most intelligent and amiable woman, was one of the Walcotts, of Windsor, in Connecticut, a family of importance in the history of that State.

This was the stock from which General Wadsworth sprung, and he proved his descent by the intrepidity and vigor of his character, as well as by that frank courtesy of manners and princely generosity which always distinguished him.

He received the first rudiments of his education at the common schools of Geneseo, although much of his youth must have been given to those rough employments in the open air which the border-life of those days required, even of the sons of rich fathers. Our esteemed friend and associate, Henry L. Pierson, remembers him well when he was a boy of twelve or thirteen, and made a visit to New York in company with his Uncle William. They had come all the way on horseback, driving a herd of cattle, and Wadsworth was then a hardy, vigorous stripling, intelligent, manly, and self-possessed.

He entered Hamilton College, near Utica ; but after a

short residence there, went to Harvard, where he remained a longer time, but was never graduated. About
the year 1829 he became a student of law at Yale, where
he stayed a few months, and then continued his course
with Mr. Webster, at Boston, and finished it in the office
of McKeon & Deniston, at Albany. He was, in due time,
called to the bar, but he never practised law as a profes-
sion. He preferred to assist his father in the care of the
family estate, which had been increased by the property
devised by his Uncle William, who died a bachelor, in
1833.

Wadsworth was married about this time to Miss
Wharton, of Philadelphia, a lady whose charms of mind
and person are so well known and so distinguished that I
may be pardoned for alluding to them here. They went
abroad soon after their marriage, and upon his return
Wadsworth applied himself with great spirit and success
to agricultural affairs. In 1842, he was elected President
of the State Society, and he always manifested a lively
interest in its prosperity. He repeatedly took prizes from
this and the County Society for the excellence of his farm
stock.

In 1844, he had the misfortune to lose his most worthy
father, and was thus left in sole charge of the greater part
of the property, embracing, in addition to his own share,
the estates of his two sisters.

He continued to make Geneseo his chief residence, and was induced, both by self-interest and affection, to promote its prosperity by every means in his power. Among other generous acts, he caused the works which supply the village with water to be constructed. He was intending to erect a building there for the purposes of the literary institution which his father had founded, when the breaking out of the war prevented the execution of the project, which, however, he provided for in his will.

He made another visit to Europe, with his family, in 1854; and shortly after his return purchased a house in Sixteenth street, in this city, which he made his permanent town residence.

On the 1st of March, 1856, he was elected a member of our Association, upon the nomination of Frederic S. Cozzens. He was not a very frequent visitor at the Club, although his absence was occasioned by no want of sympathy in our objects or regard for our members.

I now approach the time when Wadsworth's name became interwoven with the history of the Nation. Until now he had been chiefly known as a wealthy landholder—a hospitable country gentleman—a leading agriculturist. But the day had come which was to test the metal of every man's character. None came out of the furnace purer and brighter than his.

Let me attempt to describe him as those who knew

him best remember him to have been at that time. And let me first speak of his home in Geneseo, for this is necessary, that we may understand the purity of his motives, the greatness of his sacrifices, and the value of his example.

His country house, as it has been described to me by one of our most honored landscape artists, was large, but not ostentatious—embosomed in trees, and commanding, on its western side, a prospect of the beautiful valley of the Genesee, which, with its glimpses of sparkling water, its cultivated fields shut in by rich masses of foliage, and its scattered groups of oaks and elms, partook of the character of an English landscape, and reminded our artist friend of the famous view of the valley of the Thames from Richmond Hill. All these trees were parts of the primeval forest, which were preserved by the pioneer who first opened these solitudes, and had been protected since with pride and reverence by his descendants. Near the mansion was the home-farm of two thousand acres, which received the special attention of Wadsworth, and was well stocked with flocks and herds. Beyond and around, in Livingston and the neighboring counties, lay the leased lands of the estate, a domain, altogether, of fifteen thousand acres, and which, if regarded as one tract, is as large as some German principality.

I may not intrude upon the interior of the homestead, made charming by all that wealth, and taste, and affection could collect—books, pictures, music—the conversation of intelligent guests, and the exercise of graceful and refined hospitality. Here Wadsworth lived, in the midst of numerous, contented, and thriving tenants, two-thirds of whom, or their fathers, had also been the tenants of the first James Wadsworth, and thus proved, by their continuing the relation, the justice and liberality of their landlords.

I will not attempt to give a minute analysis of the character of our friend, but only to describe some of its more striking qualities. One of these seems to me to have been his direct, straightforward manliness. He never knew fear himself, and he despised all cowards. He was also eminently true and just. He hated all shams, and loved whatever was open, frank, and genuine. Perhaps he might have seemed to some a little unsympathetic—a little wanting in tenderness. But this arose from absent-mindedness or the preoccupation of engrossing business. There was an inner source of gentleness and sympathy in his nature which they discovered who knew him best, and saw him at times when the secret doors of the heart were unlocked. That he was thoroughly benevolent and generous is proved, not only by the alacrity and profusion with which he contributed to the Irish famine fund and other public and splendid charities, but also by the readiness with which, when the crops failed, he constantly forgave the rent to those small farmers who paid in kind, and thus quietly abridged his own income to the extent, sometimes, of tens of thousands of dollars.

Wadsworth had excellent natural powers of mind, but little cultivation. His intellectual ability developed rapidly in the latter years of his life. He was an original thinker. His judgment was always clear and sound; but he disliked the details of business and the petty cares of an office. He seized with great quickness the point of a law question, or any other matter which was the subject of his reading or conversation. He also was a capital judge of character, and had the art, which distinguishes many leading minds, of sifting the knowledge of those who engaged in discussions with him, by putting a few pointed questions. No one had more tact than he in talking with the farmers of his neighborhood. He rode about among them on his small pony in the most simple and unpretending manner, and his advice had always an important influence in forming and directing their opinions.

He was entirely free from all false pride. He never, directly or indirectly, boasted of his wealth or his connections. In his manners he was simple, cordial, and unaf-

3

fected. Mr. Lothrop Motley says of him, in a letter which I have read, "I have often thought and spoken of him as the true, original type of the American gentleman —not the pale, washed-out copy of the European aristocrat." In his dress and equipage he observed a simplicity which was almost Spartan. He had no trinkets or curiosities of the toilet. He was extremely temperate in eating and drinking, and despised all the epicureanism of the table.

He was now in the flower of his age. His figure was tall, well proportioned, and firmly knit. The glance of his gray eye was keen and determined. His Roman features were well rounded, and his hair, which had become prematurely white, added to the nobility of his expression.

Such is an imperfect, outline sketch of the man and of his home in Geneseo, as they appeared in the autumn of 1860, when the great Conspiracy, which had for many years been plotting at the South to destroy the National Government, proceeded from seditious language to treasonable acts, and finally dared to inaugurate flagrant and detestable Civil War. James Wadsworth took at once the most open, manly, and decided stand on the side of the Union. From that moment till the day of his death he postponed all private affairs to public duties, and devoted his time, his thoughts, his wealth, and all the

power which his position gave him to the service of his
country. To this he was impelled by his political principles, no less than his personal character. He had come
of old Federalist stock, and learned from his father to
respect the Constitution and the National Government
which the people had created under it. So long ago as
1848 he supported the Free Soil party, which had proposed his name as a District Elector. He was consistent
and persevering afterwards in his efforts on the same
side. In 1856 he received the nomination of State
Elector from the Republicans, and now, in November,
1860, he was chosen a District Elector for Lincoln and
Hamlin.

He owned immense tracts of lands and had numerous
tenants, and this, to a superficial observer, might seem
likely to have diverted his sympathies towards the
Southern Slaveholders. He was also connected, by the
marriage of one of his sisters, with a noble British family,
and his associates and intimate friends had been chiefly
formed among the wealthy classes and in circles where
the fires of patriotism were burning very low, if they had
not gone out altogether. Some of his closest friends were
indeed representatives of the best Southern society—men
possessing that refined and winning manner, the faint
tradition of Huguenot politeness, which seems, in a few
instances, to have survived the adverse influences that

surrounded it, and which has been nowhere more unduly praised than at the North. But notwithstanding all these hindrances, Wadsworth remained a true, brave, Northern Democrat. Mr. Lothrop Motley, in the letter from which I have already quoted, says of him : "He believed, honestly, frankly, and unhesitatingly in democracy, as the only possible government for our hemisphere, and as the inevitable tendency of the whole world, so far as it is able to shake off the fetters of former and present tyrannies. He honored and believed in the people with his whole heart, and it is for this reason the people honored and believed in him." . . . "It has always seemed to me," Mr. Motley adds, "that he was the truest and most thoroughly loyal American I ever knew ; and this, to my mind, is his highest eulogy, feeling as I do how immeasurably higher the political and intellectual level of America is than that of any other country in the world !"

No other man than Wadsworth valued his fellow-beings more for the high qualities of mind and heart, and, I may add, strong right arms which God had given them, and less for their clothes, their trivial accomplishments, or the company they kept. No other man than he more thoroughly despised that counterfeit chivalry whose vow of mercy was satisfied by assaulting unarmed men with swords and pistols, and of charity by squandering money borrowed of others, and never to be repaid. He had opposed the extension of slavery in the territories, and he befriended the negro as he did any other unhappy human being who needed his assistance. For this he was called by that name which seems to some persons the most opprobrious which party ingenuity can invent—the name of " Abolitionist." Perhaps the application of this name to him may add another to those examples in history, where that which was devised as the instrument of shame afterwards became the badge of immortal honor. Wadsworth saw with his clear eye that a deadly struggle had now begun between systems of society entirely repugnant to each other—between the civilized democracy of the nineteenth century and that ferocious spirit of bastard feudalism which, strangely enough, has found a more congenial home on the banks of the Mississippi than it had ever enjoyed on the Neva or the Danube. No charms of social intercourse, no claims of private friendship, obscured the clearness of his vision on this point. He attributed at once to the Southern conspirators a spirit of determined aggression— a calculating, comprehensive treason, which Northern optimists were at first reluctant to admit. He saw that the laws of population and the irresistible opinion of the world forbade them from delaying an enterprise which their mad ambition had long before planned, and that all temporizing measures on our part would be idiotic and pusillanimous.

Accordingly, in that *Comédie Larmoyante*, gotten up by crafty Virginia politicians, and misnamed the Peace Conference, upon whose doors should have been written Claudian's words:

" Mars gravior sub pace latet,"
Under the show of peace a sterner war lies hidden—

in that assembly, in which he took his seat on the 8th of February, 1861, he wasted no time in speeches, but constantly voted against all measures that seemed to jeopardize the honor and independence of the loyal States. On the 17th of February, upon his motion, the delegation of New York virtually resolved to vote No upon the chief sections of the report of the committee which summed up the action of the Conference, and the State of New York was spared the mortification of assenting to overtures which weakened the position of the North, while they failed to propitiate the Southern conspirators.

For the time was now at hand when the action of deliberative bodies was to be of no account, and the safety of the Nation to depend upon military measures alone. Fort Sumter was attacked and captured. The soldiers of Massachusetts were assaulted in the streets of Baltimore. The railroad communication with the capital

was interrupted, and the supplies for the troops there
were nearly cut off. In respect to this latter danger, the
clear, practical mind of Wadsworth seized at once the
difficulties of the situation, and devised the remedy.
With great promptness and energy, he caused two vessels to be loaded at New York, on his own account, with
provisions for the army, and accompanied them to Annap-
olis, attending personally to their delivery. During that
interval of great anxiety between the first demonstration
of the enemy against Washington and the commencement
of General McDowell's campaign, Wadsworth was in
constant communication with Lieutenant-General Scott,
and was employed by him in executing delicate and
important commissions. But he was not content with
the performance of duties which, however difficult and
responsible, made his example less valuable than the
more dangerous service of the field. He soon determined
to enter upon this, notwithstanding the sacrifices it in-
volved. Let us remember that he was now considerably
past the military age ; that his private affairs were numerous and engrossing ; that he was able to give wise counsel
and large pecuniary aid to Government, and fulfil, in
this way, every duty which the most exacting patriotism
might be supposed to require. He had, as we have seen,
a home made attractive by every thing which wealth and
taste and the love of friends could supply. His children

were just coming into the active duties of life, and while
they needed his careful supervision, their affection and
high promise made the parting from them all the more
difficult and trying. Wadsworth resisted all these temp-
tations and rejected all these excuses. In June, 1861, he
became a volunteer aid on the staff of General McDowell,
and fought his first battle in the disastrous affair of Bull
Run. His intimate friends declared, when they heard of
his resolution to take military service, that this was
equivalent to the sacrifice of his life. They knew his
bravery was so impetuous that he would court every
peril and exposure, and that he would never survive the
war. These predictions, alas! were too surely to be
realized, but not until a later day. They were, indeed,
very nearly fulfilled at Bull Run. Nobody was more
conspicuous than Wadsworth in every post of danger.
He had a horse shot under him in his efforts to rally the
panic-stricken troops. He seized the colors of the New
York Fourteenth, and adjured that brave regiment to
stand up for the old flag. He was one of the last to
leave the field, and was most active in restoring order
on the retreat, and in assisting, at Fairfax Court-House,
to preserve the government property and to relieve the
wounded.

In the organization of the National Army, Governor
Morgan, supposing he had a right to propose the names

of two Major-Generals from this State, sent Wadsworth's and Dix's to the President. We were entitled, however, to only one, and the grade was given to General Dix. Afterwards, in the summer of 1861, Wadsworth was made a Brigadier.

Whatever may be the judgment of intelligent critics upon the expediency of taking generals from civil life, and however unsatisfactory they may consider the reasons which influence the Government in making such appointments, it is admitted by all that Wadsworth received his commission with diffidence, and that his genius, which was essentially military, coupled with his attention to his duties, soon made him an efficient officer. His brigade was attached to the Army of the Potomac, and stationed in the advance, near Upton's Hill. He lay there during the autumn of 1861 and the succeeding winter, impatient at the delay of the Commander-in-Chief in moving upon Manassas, and always insisting upon what has since been proved to be true, that the enemy's force there was for a long time too weak to resist any serious attack upon it, if we had made one.

In March, 1862, General Wadsworth was appointed Military Governor of Washington, and for nine months discharged the very delicate and responsible duties of that office with great satisfaction to the Government. A

4

competent writer, who served under him, says, that "while he gave the citizens all the liberties consistent with public safety, he took vigorous measures against traitors, spies, blockade-runners, and kidnappers. He seized the slave-pen, discharged the captives, and permanently established the rule that no negro should be taken out of the District of Columbia, under color of the Fugitive Slave Law, without an examination on the part of the military authorities respecting the loyalty of the master." The same writer adds, that "great pains were taken by General Wadsworth to facilitate the change of these people from bondage to freedom. He organized a contraband bureau, established permanent quarters, taught the poor blacks how to work for themselves, and made the confiscated goods of the blockade supply their wants. Amid political and military embarrassments, he succeeded in pioneering the way to practical emancipation while commanding the fortifications and twenty-four thousand troops."

In the autumn of 1862, and while he was still in command of Washington, he received the Union nomination for Governor of New York. This had been offered to him, in 1848, by the Free-Soil Democrats, and again, in 1856, by the Republicans, but he had declined it on both occasions. He now thought it to be his duty to accept the position, and went into the canvass, but was defeated by Mr. Seymour by a majority of ten thousand seven hundred and fifty-two votes.

After nine months of service at Washington, General Wadsworth applied to the Government for more active duty. They granted his request, and, in December, 1862, ordered him to report to Major-General Reynolds, then in command of the First Corps. General Reynolds gave him his First Division, and this he led, with great gallantry, at Fredericksburg and Chancellorsville.

The experience of the last four years has proved the truth of the assertion of military men, that War is a Science which must be studied like any other, and that civilians cannot be extemporized into generals. It must be confessed, however, that the genius of some laymen eminently fits them for command, and a campaign or two may supply the want of early professional study. As I have already stated, Wadsworth seems to have been one of these natural soldiers. He was very successful in gaining the love of his men. His high sense of justice and true republican respect for manliness, wherever he found it, soon convinced them that if they did their duty they should be rewarded. They knew, too, that he made their comfort his constant study. These qualities endeared him greatly to his troops, and when, before the battle of Fredericksburg, he rode with his staff unexpectedly into the encampment of his old brigade, the soldiers of all the four regiments rushed tumultuously towards him and made the skies ring with their shouts of welcome.

But there was another and a better reason why his soldiers loved him, and also why he was always a reliable officer: he was so cool and collected under fire. "He had a habit," says an intelligent writer, who saw him at the front just before his death, "of riding about the foremost line, and even among his skirmishers, which somewhat unnecessarily exposed his life. He knew very well how to handle his division, and he knew how to hold a line of battle—how to order and lead a charge— how to do the plain work which he liked best; and at Gettysburg he showed how much a plucky, tenacious leader can do with a handful of troops in keeping back and making cautious an overwhelming force of the enemy. He was pertinacious; did not like to give up or back out; and was not a man safely to be pressed, even by a force much superior to his own."

General Meade writes of him: "The moral effect of his example, his years and high social position, his distinguished personal gallantry and daring bravery, all tended to place him in a most conspicuous position, and to give him an influence over the soldiers which few other men possess."

And General Humphreys, General Meade's chief of

staff, in speaking of the qualities he showed on the field on which he lost his life, writes: "In the two days of desperate fighting that followed our crossing the Rapidan, he was conspicuous *beyond all others* for his gallantry—prompter than all others in leading his troops again and again into action. In all these combats he literally *led* his men, who, inspired by his heroic bearing, continually renewed the contest, which, but for him, they would have yielded."

This is high praise, and from the most competent sources, to be given to a man who had never been under fire until he had passed his fifty-third year, and whose life had been occupied in quiet agricultural pursuits. It was the blood of the old Puritan Captain which tingled in his veins in those days of trial: better than that, it was the inextinguishable love of country—the reverence for Right and Truth—the inborn hatred of every thing false, and mean, and treacherous, which made him content to exchange the delights of such a home as I have attempted to describe for the unspeakable horrors of the battle-field.

It may well be supposed that with qualities like these he was not allowed to remain inactive in the campaign which succeeded the battles of Fredericksburg and Chancellorsville. At Gettysburg he commanded the First Division of the First Corps until the fall of General Reynolds, when he assumed charge of the corps. Before that, however, his division had received the brunt of the enemy's attack. It went into action at nine in the morning, and continued under fire until four in the afternoon, suffering heavier loss than any other in the army. He had several horses shot under him, and he animated the fight everywhere by his noble presence. At the council of war held after the victory, Wadsworth, who, as the temporary commander of a corps, had a seat at the board, with great modesty, but with decided earnestness, favored the pursuit of the enemy, but his advice was overruled and Lee escaped.

After General Grant was ordered to the Eastern Division, Wadsworth was constantly employed in assisting in the arrangements for the present campaign. Before it was undertaken, however, and about the beginning of the present year, he was sent upon special service to the Mississippi Valley, and made an extensive tour through the Western and Southwestern States. It was on the eve of his departure that he made to the paymaster from whom he had always drawn his pay, the remarkable declaration that he desired to have his accounts with Government kept by one and the same officer, because it was his purpose, at the close of the war, to call for an accurate statement of all the money he should have received, and then to give it, whatever might be the amount, to some permanent institution, founded for the relief of invalid soldiers. "This is the least invidious way," said he, "in which I can refuse pay for fighting for my country in her hour of danger."

When General Grant commenced his present campaign, Wadsworth was placed in command of the Fourth Division of the Fifth Corps, which was composed of his old division of the First Corps, with the addition of the Third Brigade. He crossed the Rapidan on Wednesday, the 4th of May. On the 6th, the battle of the Wilderness was fought, in which our friend was mortally wounded. This event, and its attendant circumstances, are described in simple and touching language by his son, Captain Craig Wadsworth, in a letter which is published in Mr. Allen's Memorial. Captain Wadsworth was attached to the cavalry division, which was guarding the wagon train ; but, by permission of his commanding officer, he went to the front, and remained with his father for two or three hours on the morning of the memorable 6th, and while the fight was going on.

It seems, from that account, that General Wadsworth's command had been engaged for several hours on the evening of the 5th, and had lost heavily. Early the next morning General Hancock ordered it again into action, on the right of the Second Corps. Wadsworth charged repeatedly with his division and carried an important point, which he was unable to hold, owing to the superior force of the enemy. He was afterwards re-enforced, and, with six brigades, made three or four other assaults upon Hill's Corps, which was the one opposed to him. In these assaults he fought with the greatest gallantry, having two horses killed under him. At eleven o'clock, General Hancock ordered him to withdraw, and there was a lull in the battle until about noon, when Longstreet precipitated his force upon Wadsworth's left and drove back Ward's brigade, at that point, in some confusion. Wadsworth thereupon immediately threw forward his second line, composed of his own division, and formed it on the plank-road, at right angles with his original position. It was while trying to hold this line, with his own division, then reduced to about sixteen hundred men, that his third horse was shot under him, and he was himself struck in the head by a bullet. The enemy were charging at the time, and took the ground before the General could be removed. He was captured and carried, while he was probably in a state of insensibility, to one of the rebel hospitals. No medical skill could save his life. He lingered from Friday afternoon until Sunday morning, and then yielded his brave spirit into the hands of its Maker.

Thus died James Wadsworth, in the fifty-seventh year of his age, and in the full strength of his manhood.

Many a true, and brave, and noble soldier fell on that
bloody field, but none truer, or braver, or nobler than
he. Many a patriot consummated there the long record
of his sacrifices, but none left a brighter and purer record
of sacrifices than he. In this war, which has been illus-
trated by so many instances of heroism, it seems almost
unjust to compare one man's services with another's ;
and Wadsworth, with his unaffected modesty, and his
reverence for worth wherever it existed, if his spirit
could sit in judgment on our words, would rebuke us
for attributing to him a more genuine loyalty than that
which animated many a poor private who fell by his
side. But when we remember how entirely impossible
it was in his case that his worldly advantages should
have been increased by military service, and how often
it is that a mixture of motives impels men in general to
undertake it, we feel that we can give our praise to him
with fuller hearts, in no unstinted measure, and with no
reservations or perplexing doubts.

As he lay upon the field, in the midst of the dead and
the dying, in that awful interval between the retreat of
his own men and the advance of the enemy, if any gleam
of consciousness was vouchsafed to him, may we not
hope that the recollection of his noble fidelity to his
country assuaged the bitterness of that solemn hour ?

5

"Who is the happy warrior?" asks a famous English
poet; and the poet answers, he is the happy warrior

"Whom neither shape of danger can dismay,
Nor thought of tender happiness betray:

*   *   *   *   *

Who, whether praise of him must walk the earth
Forever, and to noble deeds give birth,
Or he must go to dust without his fame,
And leave a dead, unprofitable name,
Finds comfort in himself and in his cause;
And while the mortal mist is gathering, draws
His breath in confidence of Heaven's applause.
This is the happy warrior, this is he
Whom every man in arms should wish to be!"

My friends, will it violate the proprieties of this occasion; will it seem to be turning our thoughts too far
from him whose life and services we so gratefully commemorate, if we seek, in his example, some influence
which may strengthen our own patriotism and confirm
our hesitating feet in that path which he trod with such
unfaltering step?

We claim, in this Association, to be animated by
better motives than money-getting or pleasure-seeking.
We try to encourage a spirit of philosophic inquiry and
the study of literature and art. These are noble objects.
But is it not true that, instead of aiding and stimulating,
they sometimes take the place of that love of country
which is so much higher and nobler than they? Is it not

true that everywhere in this Nation, even in this moment of supreme trial, when the Republic needs the best thoughts and the most sagacious counsels as well as the life-blood of her sons, there are men of distinguished position, of large experience, ripe learning, and varied accomplishments, who are still intent upon their books and their pictures, and who abandon public affairs to pretenders making a trade of politics, and having no more intelligence or learning than they have patriotism or virtue?

If there be thousands of men who, like Wadsworth, are willing to give their lives and all that they hold most dear and precious for their country, is it too much to ask that we should sacrifice in her service a little of our time and our comfort—a little of the leisure that we devote to literary and artistic pursuits—a little of the luxurious ease of our pleasant studies?

"Too much to ask," do I say? What would be all the consolations of philosophy — all the delights of poetry—all the charms of books, and pictures, and intellectual converse, if the administration of our political affairs should be surrendered to knaves and tricksters, if chicanery should take the place of statesmanship, if our country, the loving mother of us all, should stand ashamed and degraded before the nations, dishonored by her children, all the brightness of her raiment tarnished, and the light of glory burning no longer in her eagle eyes!

My friends, let us renew our vows of allegiance to her over Wadsworth's bleeding body; let us swear to hold her, next after God, first in our heart of hearts; to devote to her the best fruits of our studies, the most exquisite works of our hands—to defend her against all assaults; to magnify her in the face of her enemies, and, finally, if she should demand the sacrifice, to lay down our lives in her service!

MR. COZZENS'S

EULOGY

ON

COLONEL PORTER.

It has been the custom of our honored Institution, from its beginning, to pay some brief tribute to the memory of its departed members, as year after year separates name after name from its fraternal roll. It is a beautiful custom, and one peculiarly suited to this Association, which, being necessarily limited in numbers, feels the more keenly the loss of any one who has been a part and agent of itself. If the qualifications of a new member are so closely determined, both in the Board of Admissions and by the open vote of the Club, that we may feel assured that there is nothing in the mind, the character, or the career of the candidate to conflict with the objects of "The Century," nor to mar its harmonious movements in obedience to the organic law which called it into being, how much the more do we estimate the character of a member who has been for many years bound to us by every social tie, and endeared to us by every quality that lends dignity and grace, even to the Association itself?

At the annual meeting of next month we shall commemorate the eighteenth anniversary of "The Century." A glance at its original purport may not be uninteresting, in connection with the subject of this discourse. On January 13, 1847, the first meeting was held. It was then "deemed expedient to form an association of gentlemen of the city of New York and its vicinity, engaged or interested in letters or the fine arts, in order to bring them into more frequent, friendly, and social intercourse; and, at the same time, afford them opportunities of consultation in regard to the fine arts of this country—a subject in which all felt the deepest interest." It was then proposed that the Association should consist of one hundred members. Mr. Edgar S. Van Winkle suggested that, from the number of its members, it should be called "The Century." This happy title was adopted, and although we have grown out of the limits of the specified number embraced in the title, yet, in honor to the original founders, we bear the name still.

It would be a grateful task to trace the history of "The Century" from its inception to the present time. The illustrious men, of all countries, who have found access to its congenial climate, speak of it in terms too flattering to be repeated here. Its objects have never been corrupted by any influences strong enough to move it from the broad base upon which it was organically established. When innovation attempted to change its purpose, it moved a little, but swung back into its old courses, as if it had been the very pendulum of conservatism. For in the harmonious intercourse which brings together gentlemen of taste and cultivation to discuss subjects connected with Letters—with Sculpture or Painting—with Progressive Science, or those Studies dear to the learned professions; in such an intellectual convention there is no place for petty rivalries or narrow schemes. On the contrary, such an association not only ennobles, elevates, dignifies the social intercourse of its members, but its influence extends beyond the limits of itself; it enriches the land with its silent but powerful efforts in favor of correct taste and all the beautiful manifestations of art, and even carries into every action of familiar life a quiet charm, of which we are scarcely aware until we begin to consider from whence this influence is derived.

Is it then surprising that with this sweet fraternal feeling growing and clustering, year after year, within and around and about us, that *here*, much more than in ordinary life, we should feel the loss we have sustained when we behold an empty space where once stood the animated form; where once we met the

6

happy smile; where once we responded to the joyous voice?

Is it unmanly to remember that several familiar faces are no longer seen at our festivals? When the first eulogy pronounced in "The Century," over the lamented Seymour, was hushed, was it not "a sad but pleasing thought" that we had preserved the brief memorial of his fellowship with us? Was there not even a more grateful feeling that we had had the forethought to do so, when, only a few years afterwards, we assembled upon a similar occasion, to listen to a passing tribute to the memory of Robert Kelly, the second member "The Century" had lost—himself the eulogist of the first?*

Since that time many names have been added to the roll of the departed. And as the mortuary record lengthens—for who can tell whose name shall be the next inscribed upon it?—there is a pleasing consciousness that we, in turn, shall be remembered by those that survive us—at our gatherings—at our meetings for business—at our festivals; whenever there shall be a "Century"

---

* Daniel Seymour, the first Secretary of "The Century," was a gentleman of the finest literary tastes and attainments. He, and Robert Kelly were fellow-students at Columbia College. Kelly was the more distinguished in public life as a leader in those benevolent institutions which have had so marked an influence upon our municipal history. Both were eminently beloved in private as in public life. The unobtrusive merit of the one, with the active benevolence of the other, formed a beautiful contrast.

assemblage, large or small—that there we shall not be
forgotten !

It is scarcely necessary to recall to the minds of a
majority of the members present, that our late friend
and associate was the only son of "that brave soldier
of the War of 1812," General Peter B. Porter. It is
due to the memory of the son that this memoir should
also embrace a brief sketch of the father, particularly as
no reliable history of the war in which he bore so distinguished a part has yet been written.

Among the earliest of the pioneers in Western New
York, were two brothers, Augustus and Peter B. Porter,
sons of Dr. Joshua Porter, of Salisbury, Connecticut.

This Dr. Joshua Porter, the grandfather of Peter A.
Porter, left behind him an autobiography, in manuscript,
written in his ninety-first year, from which it appears
that he was born in Wyndham, Connecticut, June 26,
1730; graduated at Yale College in 1752 or 1753; was
educated as a physician, and removed to Salisbury, Connecticut, in November, 1757. For twenty-two years he
was a member of the Connecticut Assembly, and sat in
the lower house during forty-five sessions; was ·ap-
pointed Judge of Probate in 1774, and held the office
until 1812. In the Revolutionary War he commanded a
regiment, which was for some time stationed at the then
important point on the Hudson, Peekskill, forming one

of the defences of the river; and he was afterwards in the battle of Saratoga and at the memorable surrender of Burgoyne, October 16, 1777. He was also a member of the Connecticut Convention assembled to ratify the Constitution of the United States, in 1788; and his vote, as Colonel Joshua Porter, is recorded, January 9th of that year, in the affirmative.

He was esteemed to be a man of vigorous mind, even in extreme old age, and his life had been as active as it was blameless. His two sons were well educated, and carried with them into the western wilderness the customs, the training, and the experience of cultivated life.

The younger brother, Peter B. Porter, was born at Salisbury, Connecticut, in 1773; graduated at Yale College in 1791, and studied law with Judge Reeve, of Litchfield. At this time the Great Holland Purchase, as it was then called, and has since been known, stimulated the enterprising and the intrepid in all parts of the country. This vast tract of three millions six hundred thousand acres, originally purchased of the State of Massachusetts by Robert Morris, the great financier of the Revolution, and by him sold, in 1792 and 1793, to Hermon Le Roy, John Linklaen, Gerrit Boon, and others, in trust for certain capitalists in Holland, who had furnished the money, comprises the whole or part of the counties of Allegany, Wyoming, Genesee, Orleans, Cat-

taraugus, Erie, Niagara, and Chautauque. To this un-
broken region, "the wild lands of Western New York,"
the brothers Porter emigrated in the year 1793. In an
address prepared thirty-eight years afterwards, for the
Euglossian Society, of Geneva College, the younger
brother speaks "of entering the interminable forests of
the West at the German Flats, at Mohawk, which was
then the extreme verge of civilized improvements. The
only evidences of civilized life consisted of some half-
dozen log-huts at Utica, and the same again at Canandaigua. Besides these, there were a few miserable cabins
sprinkled along the road, at a distance of five to ten
miles apart, where the traveller might look, not as now,
for comfort or for rest, but for the sheer necessities of
continuing his journey."

In 1795, the young pioneer, then in his twenty-second
year, commences the practice of law at Canandaigua; in
1797, he begins his official life as County Clerk for the
county of Ontario; in 1802, he is elected member of
the State Legislature; and in 1808 and 1810, is elected
to Congress. In the latter year he removes to Black
Rock, where he has large possessions, and in the year
following is prominently engaged upon two of the most
important subjects that then occupied the public mind,
and which have ever since exercised a marked influence, not only upon the interests of the State, but upon

the whole country. The first was his appointment, by
act of Legislature of the State of New York (April 8,
1811), on a commission "for taking into consideration
all matters relating to Inland Navigation." It is impossible to over-estimate the value of this, the greatest Board
of Commissioners the State of New York ever selected.
It does not lessen, in the eyes of an admiring posterity,
the high, patriotic, and sagacious character of this wise
body of counsellors, when it is remembered that they
were not selected with any reference to party measures.
The very mention of these eminent men at once recalls
the Empire State in its proudest days, as well as its
most disinterested legislators. It is a pleasure to repeat
their names—Gouverneur Morris, Stephen Van Rensse-
laer, De Witt Clinton, William North, Simeon De Witt,
Thomas Eddy, Peter B. Porter, Robert R. Livingston,
and last, not least, Robert Fulton! It is to this commission that we owe the policy which gave our State
that teeming cornucopia of the West—the Erie Canal!

> O forethought shrewd! O stretch of human mind!
> O genius born to bless, not curse mankind!
> That with prophetic skill (like him, the blest)
> Saw the rich Canaan of the teeming West!
> And that the States their chiefest boon should know,
> Struck the bare rock, and bade the waters flow.
> What had the East to boast, not having this?
> On ocean's cheek what touch like Erie's kiss?
> Lo, the broad West his genius shall proclaim!
> And famished Europe murmur Clinton's name!

That we owe to the inventive genius of De Witt
Clinton the first thought of this great public work, the
greatest the world has ever seen, is no less true than
that we owe to the commission, that supported him in
those trying days, a kindred debt of gratitude.

In the same year (1811), but following his action
upon this commission, Peter B. Porter filled the important post, in Congress, of Chairman of the Committee
on Foreign Relations. The Berlin and Milan decrees of
Napoleon (the Continental Policy, as it was called), and
the no less stringent policy of Great Britain, embraced
in the "Orders in Council," had almost totally destroyed
our commerce. But not only this, the free right to the
high seas, the germ of all the policy that from that time
to this has been dear to every American heart; the sense
of injustice that had already swept away the Tripolitan
tribute under Preble and Decatur (as it has more recently
the sound dues demanded by the countrymen of Hamlet);
the right to sail a ship, in any sea, without interference
from any powers, save those of Divine Providence, at
that time had begun to excite the deepest interest. These
subjects of international polity were somewhat complicated by the embargo and non-intercourse acts of our own
country.

All these matters being before the Committee of the
House on Foreign Relations, of which Peter B. Porter

was Chairman, were speedily brought to a point. France having repealed the Berlin and Milan decrees, so far as they concerned the United States, Great Britain demanded still higher authority over the high seas in relation to the same power. In response to this the Committee reported, through their Chairman, resolutions recommending the increase of the military force, the fitting up of war vessels, the allowancing of merchant vessels to arm in self-defence, and such other measures as were necessary to maintain the position the United States had taken.

In the records we find that the speech of the Chairman, Peter B. Porter, introducing these resolutions, was marked by "great ability, firm and energetic in its tone, yet temperate and judicious." The resolutions were adopted December 19, 1811.* Immediately afterwards he resigned his seat in Congress. And although tendered a Brigadier's commission in the regular army, he declined it in favor of a commission from his own State as Quartermaster-General. From this period his active military life begins. "To trace his military career," says the author of the Holland Purchase, "from battle-field to battle-field, would be to write a history of a large portion of the war upon the Niagara frontier."

* Hildreth, Vol. III., sec. 2, p. 226.

It is to be regretted that we have not a complete, reliable history of our last struggle with England. It is, to be sure, "a spotted field:" and perhaps (to many) a bare exhibition of the record would be not pleasing. There were many who objected to that war: there was much legislative interference ; there were some conventions in session whose proceedings amounted to very little; and perhaps some trifling with fire-arms at Detroit and Bladensburg ; but why should a respect for the feelings of a few imperfect-minded men, in some narrow strips and shreds of this great nation, be a barrier to a publication that would place in bold relief the heroic character of the real men of that time ?

The War of 1812 was, at the same time, the shortest, as well as one of the most important wars that ever occupied the attention of mankind. That it was brief, we have only to consider that the Declaration of War was proclaimed June 18, 1812, and that the Declaration of Peace was ratified at Washington February 17, 1815— say two years and eight months, save one day. That it was important, the freedom of the high-seas will witness. That it destroyed the power of Great Britain upon those blue waters, is now a matter of history. It was a battle fought for all mankind as to the right of a common highway. It was a battle for a right-of-way over a briny common that a modern king of Great Britain had no

7

more authority to control than one of its ancient kings had to bid, "come no farther."*

In the early part of the contest Hull's surrender at Detroit had turned the direction of the war to the Niagara frontier, as the most vulnerable point along the lines. As we have seen, General Porter was at this time residing at Black Rock, where he had large possessions. But his active, energetic mind did not permit him to remain at home during the first indications of battle. We find him "twice leading the van" in General Smythe's unfortunate army of invasion in 1812, and his sarcastic comments upon this futile attempt led to a duel between him and his superior officer. In 1813, the British surprise Black Rock, and he narrowly escapes being captured in his own house. The result of his escape is the capture by him, in turn, of the capturers of Black Rock— Lieutenant-Colonel Bishop and his forces. We hear of him as taking an active part in the Sackett's Harbor expedition; in the contemplated attack of Montreal; in the attack and capture of Little York (now Toronto). In 1814, he joins Major-General Jacob Brown with a brigade of thirty-five hundred men, composed of New York and Pennsylvania Volunteers, with a portion of

* The intense feeling of this time, as well as the popular sentiment, is to be found in the brief abstract of General Porter's speech, in Hildreth's History of the United States, Second Series, Vol. III., p. 260, to the end of the chapter.

the Indians of the Six Nations, particularly the Seneca
tribe, headed by those notable warriors and orators,
Corn-Planter and Red-Jacket.* It is to be remembered
that the Indians on the enemy's side were headed by
the son of Joseph Brant (Thayendanagea). The memorable battle of Chippewa followed, in which Porter
was an active and gallant, though not successful, participant. General Armstrong, in his notice of the War
of 1812, says: "General Brown detached Brigadier-
General Porter, of the New York Militia, to march
rapidly, under cover of an adjoining wood, and throw
himself between the British skirmishing party and the
main body. He succeeded in completely routing the
outposts, and was pursuing them, when he unexpectedly
found himself in presence of the *main body*, and was
obliged to retreat." This affair was commented upon
with great severity by some military critics of the day;
great cowardice was awarded to the militia, but the
gallant conduct of General Porter was greatly applauded
by all. In Major-General Brown's official report of
Chippewa, he says: "By this time Porter's command
gave way and fled in every direction, notwithstanding

* See Stone's Life of Red-Jacket, also his Life of Joseph Brant. The latter
contains a letter from Porter, descriptive of Brant's habits in England. It shows
the Mohawk chief to have been a most amiable and gentlemanly person, in
accordance with his early training (which was for the Church), notwithstanding
his natural taste for blood. But all men have their weaknesses.

his personal gallantry and great exertion to stay the
flight." But this very body of volunteers more than
redeemed themselves in the battle of Lundy's Lane and
the sortie of Fort Erie. In the terrible conflict of Lundy's
Lane. when the brave Colonel Miller had carried the
heights, and captured the key of the position, it was
Porter's volunteers that served as the supporting force;
and the details of that battle furnish the evidence how
bravely they made amends for their former lack of spirit.
A gallant officer, who was himself an actor in this battle,
in speaking of the last desperate charge that decided the
day, says: "Porter's volunteers were not excelled by
the regulars during this charge. They were soon precipitated, by their heroic commander, upon the enemy's
line, which they broke and dispersed, making many
prisoners. The enemy now seemed to be effectually
routed—they disappeared. And even at Chippewa, a
portion of these men were rallied by their commander,
and ordered forward in pursuit of the enemy, which, by
General Scott, were driven back from that hard-fought
field, and decided the conflict in our favor."*

For these various services General Porter was com-
misioned Major-General in the Regular Army of the
United States.

* Silliman's Gallop through American Scenery, p. 255.

After Lundy's Lane, the sortie from Fort Erie forms the chief point of interest in the history of the war on the Niagara frontier. This fort had been captured some time before by the Americans, had been strengthened by them materially, and was strongly garrisoned; but General Drummond, being heavily re-enforced, determined to capture it by assault, on the morning of the 15th of August, 1814. The repulse of the British, and the death of General Drummond, who was shot while exclaiming "Show no mercy!" after the capture of a bastion, are sufficiently familiar. The enemy withdrew to a safe distance for a regular siege; and, after a month's time, had advanced his parallels to within four hundred yards of the right of our lines. General Brown determined to attack him within his own defences. A rainy, foggy morning was selected for the enterprise. The command of the right wing was given to the brave Colonel Miller; the left to General Porter. Ripley held the reserve. Porter's command consisted of his volunteers, Gibson's riflemen, and the remains of the First and Twenty-third Regiments of United States Infantry. The assault was made with desperate fury. Porter carried a block-house of the enemy, in rear of Battery No. 3, by storm; made the garrison prisoners; blew up the powder magazine; and hastened to the assistance of Colonel Miller. He, in turn, had penetrated Batteries Nos. 1 and 2, and, by the aid of Porter, carried both. The result was, that the British advanced works being destroyed, and a large number of prisoners captured, as well as a heavy loss in killed and wounded, caused the works of Drummond to be abandoned. General Brown, in his report, says: "In a close action, not exceeding an hour, one thousand troops of the line, and an equal number of New York Militia, destroyed the fruits of fifty days' labor, diminished his effective force one thousand men, and forced upon him the abandonment of the siege and speedy retreat to Chippewa." And a military critic of no little renown, Major-General Sir William F. P. Napier, in his History of the War of the Peninsula, refers to it in high terms, as follows: "The sortie of Fort Erie was a brilliant achievement; the only instance in history where a besieging army was entirely broken up and routed by a single sortie."

But this gallant action was not without severe loss on our side. The three officers in command of the divisions under General Porter—Colonel Gibson, General Davis, and Lieutenant-Colonel Wood, fell mortally wounded. General Porter himself was wounded twice in the sortie. An incident, characteristic of his bravery and presence of mind, is related by his son. As he was going from one part of the field to another, during the engagement, attended only by his staff, he came

suddenly upon a party of British soldiers, about eighty
in number. Putting a bold face upon the matter, he
went up to them, and said, "That's right, my brave
fellows! surrender; I'll take care of you," at the same
time throwing down their muskets, which were piled or
stacked; but they, recovering from their surprise, picked
up their fire-arms, and no doubt would have captured
him and his staff, but for the timely appearance of a
body of Americans. The result was a brisk skirmish,
in which most of the enemy were killed or made prisoners. "With the destruction of Fort Erie, and the
removal of the troops from the Canada line, the campaign of the Army of the North, in 1814, was ended."*
In acknowledgment of his services in this war, the city
of New York presented General Porter with the freedom
of the city in a gold box; the State of New York voted
him a sword; and the thanks of the Congress of the
United States, with a gold medal, struck to commemorate the successful campaign of 1814, were presented
to the five generals who had most distinguished themselves—General Brown, General Scott, General Ripley,
General Gaines, and General Porter. In the lately published autobiography of Lieutenant-General Scott there
is but little mention of General Porter, in connection

* "Scenes in the War of 1812."—*Harper*, January, 1864.

with the battles of Chippewa and Lundy's Lane. But it is not the custom with autobiographers to permit the public mind to be diverted from the principal character, whose great deeds they are describing. Some correspondence, however, found among General Porter's papers, after his death, reveals the fact that his great services were not overlooked by the Government in 1814. He was then appointed "*Commander-in-Chief of the Army of the Frontier;*" and his commission, with the papers accompanying it, are now in the possession of his family. But the war being speedily brought to a close, he declined the merited distinction, as his services were no longer actively required.

But the exercise of his abilities for the public good did not cease with his military life. In the year following the war (1815), we find him nominated by the Governor of the State of New York, Daniel D. Tompkins, for Secretary of State. "He did not solicit the appointment," says Hammond, "his business at Black Rock, where he resided, requiring his personal attention;" and, besides, he had been the year before re-elected to Congress. His appointment, however, was confirmed by the Council; and as it may be interesting to know *why*, I quote the language used upon the occasion: "That General Peter B. Porter had honorably distinguished himself in the army on the Niagara frontier during the war; and, besides, was justly esteemed as a man of the first order of intellect." These were considered *qualifications* in 1815. It does not appear, however, that even with this flattering commendation, he served as Secretary of State; his election to Congress may have prevented his acceptance. In 1816 we still find him occupied with arduous public duties. He is appointed (by President Madison) Commissioner, under the Treaty of Ghent, to settle the boundary line between the United States and Great Britain.

For a time we lose sight of him as a public man. He married, late in life, Mrs. Letitia Grayson, a widow lady, and daughter of the late John Breckinridge, of Kentucky, formerly Attorney-General of the United States, under President Jefferson. The estimable character of this most charitable and pious lady, who died only a few brief years after her marriage, leaving a son and daughter, is so well known that it has become a matter of public record, and therefore I do not transgress the limit of propriety in speaking of her here.

The personal friend of Colonel Porter, as well as his legal adviser and executor,* who has generously furnished me with the materials he had collected for a biographical sketch for the Buffalo Historical Society, says, in a letter:

---

* Mr. Charles D. Norton, of Buffalo.

8

"I recollect her, a woman of noble presence and imperial face and form, very gracious in her manners, of wonderful capacity in the management of affairs; of a most benevolent and charitable disposition, she was the friend of the friendless and the supporter and benefactress of all worthy institutions. She was renowned in this region for her care of the poor, and her sympathy for all those in circumstances either of poverty or affliction. Her door, in the cold mornings of winter, was beset by her dependents, and they went away rejoicing in what was most necessary for them in their condition. At her decease, the local journals, the papers of Washington, New York, Philadelphia, Charleston, and Louisville, spoke of her in terms of the highest eulogy, and recorded her many virtues. Her correspondence shows her to have been the friend of Clay, Calhoun, General Scott, and the most distinguished statesmen of her time; and I find letters of condolence upon her decease from General Scott, Henry Clay, Mr. Calhoun, General Cass, Mr. Preston, Commodore Rodgers, and others; all of them expressive of the same grief for her death, and extolling those remarkable graces of mind and person for which she was distinguished above her sex.

"From such a mother Colonel Porter inherited many of his noblest traits of character, and it is not surprising that a man thus born and reared and educated should have been noticeable for the best gifts which God vouch-safes to the distinguished sons of our race."

The last important position which General Porter occupied in public affairs was that of Secretary of War, under the administration of John Quincy Adams, in 1828. It is said that this appointment was derived solely from the active influence of Mr. Clay, his personal friend and rival in debate, who fully appreciated his great shrewdness and sagacity. A contemporary, and one of the few able men that have survived this period, says, "that his administration was very able; his method excellent; being himself a business man, the routine of his department was thorough, while his official documents were marked with great elegance of style, as well as singular simplicity and clearness. He was a little deaf, but it was a great pleasure to sit beside him, upon social occasions, at table; his manners were fascinating, and his conversation happy and unaffected, although pregnant with fine thoughts and observations of the world."* From another source we learn, "that in the records of legislation, in State or Nation, there are few better specimens of eloquence than he uttered, or of compositions than those that came from his pen."†

If I have trespassed too much upon your time, in

---

* Hon. Gulian C. Verplanck.   † Holland Purchase, p. 615.

recalling these particulars, it is because a brief history of the career of the gallant father forms a portion, as it were, of the biography of his no less gallant son. We recognize the same traits of character in both, and the comparison is drawn still closer when we reflect that the hero that led the sortie of Fort Erie was then about the same age as our hero when he led the charge at the bloody battle of Cold Harbor, Virginia.

Peter Augustus Porter was born at Black Rock (now a part of Buffalo, New York), July 14, 1827. Four years afterwards, in 1831, we find, by the family record, that he becomes an orphan on the mother's side; and in 1844, a few years after the General's removal to Niagara Falls, a great concourse assembles there to pay the last tribute of respect to the hero of Fort Erie and the Niagara frontier. At the time of the death of his father, he is still a mere youth, seventeen years of age. It is due to his memory to say, that much of the care of his earlier years devolved upon his only sister, of whom he always spoke in terms of the tenderest affection.

He was prepared for college by the Rev. James Such, a graduate of Cambridge, an English gentleman, and an accomplished scholar. He entered Harvard College in August, 1842, in the Sophomore class; graduated in August, 1845; visited Europe in May, 1846; and studied for some years at Heidelberg, Berlin, and Breslau, in order to perfect himself in the usual accomplishments of a scholar and a gentleman. He returned to America in the spring of 1849, to take charge of his patrimonial estate, which was large, and situated in the counties of Erie and Niagara. In 1854 he engages in the study of the law, at Cambridge, Massachusetts; in September, 1855, he again visits Europe, and returns in May, 1857.

It would appear incumbent upon me to refer here to his immediate family relations. It is true, they form part of his domestic history; but it seems to me too delicate a task to perform now. I shall, therefore, avoid treading upon this sacred ground, and I am sure he would sanction my reticence if he were present.

Let us, rather, turn to those matters which more immediately concern his connection with "The Century." He became a member of the Association on the 9th of January, 1853.

At this time the "Journal of the Century" was in full vigor. The "Journal" was a collection of papers, contributed from time to time by the members, and read at the monthly meetings. Mr. John H. Gourlie was then the chief, and I had the honor to be junior, editor. One evening, just preceding the monthly meeting in July, 1853, Mr. Cranch placed in my hands a MS. poem, entitled "The Spirit of Beauty." It struck me then as a rare specimen of rhythmical art, and it possessed, besides,

a very subtle humoristic quality, that rare and dangerous
companion of delicate verse. When it was read its re-
ception was as flattering as its merits deserved. I was
then just acquainted with the author, and at my request
he permitted the poem to be printed in the "Knicker-
bocker" of the following month, by whose judicious
readers it was highly relished and appreciated. In
April, 1857, another poem from his pen, entitled "Arca-
dia, a Medley," was read before "The Century," and
at my request he allowed it to be published in "Put-
nam's Magazine," of May. It was not the less enjoyed
and appreciated. In 1858 he wrote the "King's Speech,"
in the great Twelfth Night festival ; and at the Twelfth
Night festival of 1859, made the "Queen's Speech,"
both of which are preserved in the archives of "The
Century." The last contribution of Colonel Porter to
"The Journal" was in 1858. It was a humorous tilt
at our ancient festivals, entitled the "Centurion's Dream."
It was subsequently printed in the "Crayon," of November, 1860. This, like all the other productions of his
pen, he had great misgivings for ; he did not think it
worth publishing. I had some difficulty in changing
his opinion, or, perhaps, his determination. In regard
to these matters, he always afforded a striking and a
pleasing contrast to many other versifiers with whom
I had the honor to be acquainted. Their pens were

not lodged in the racks before they were ready to fly into the world, to let · that great listener know what they had done. But that great listener is as discriminating as it is amiable ; and it has placed a few poems of modest merit far above the strife, the rivalry, the dust, and struggles of literary aspirants, in the poetical arena. Let us, at least, accord to Porter that he was not a contestant for the laurel crown. He looked upon the conflict from his side-box. He had learned, from the teachings of his early tutor, the Rev. James Such, who was a most accomplished scholar in versification, the full value of prosody, the longs and shorts, the rhythmical music of the old English tongue ; and he employed his lore in compositions merely for the amusement of his friends.

A beautiful elegiac poem from his hand, written in Europe, some years ago, "Upon hearing of the early death of George H. Emerson, a college friend and classmate," was republished in the "New York Times" of June 14th or 15th of this year. It is full of the tenderest pathos, and might properly be quoted here, if it did not too painfully recall the writer. In the "Wine Press" for April, 1860, a contribution from his pen appears. It purports to be a continuation of Macaulay's History ; but the writer, with that constant regard for truth which, even in fiction or in jest, always accompanies him, says of the sketches of the lives of Washington and Franklin, "they purport to be sketches for a future volume, by Macaulay;" but in the preceding paragraph he says, "*but for their authenticity I do not vouch.*" And this he does as a forewarning to the cursory reader, to be on his guard against the playful deception, which is so close to the original in *style*, that it might have deceived the most cultivated and the most observant of critics.

In the "Buffalo Commercial Advertiser" of November 19th, 1864, appears a posthumous poem, entitled "Come nearer to me, Sister," written by Porter, when only nineteen years of age. It bears all the promises of his early genius, which afterwards ripened into more perfect productions. I do not know of any American poem more tenderly pathetic than it. To any one competent to measure the latent and undeveloped powers of a highly imaginative mind—rich in treasures of learning and controlled by an exquisite taste—these few pieces will afford a curious and interesting study. The humorous verses exhibit, with every changing current of the theme, a wonderfully creative fancy, original in conception, delicate in expression, and almost as perfect in musical rhythm as some of the most elaborate essays in versification of the present time. In the elegiac lines we find the same powers of imagination developed in language of the deepest pathos; nervous, but chastened by the tenderest emotions, and elevated in accordance with the solemn character of the theme. In the imitations of Macaulay, we perceive that it is the style only of the late eminent historian that is copied. The thoughts are Porter's own; and, clothed in other language, without the trick of antithetical rhetoric, would place his powers as an analyst of character upon a par with those of the happiest writers of that class. In all things his judgment went hand in hand with his imagination; his exuberant fancy was curbed by his taste; and his erudition was only equalled by his modesty.

Nor was his knowledge in art less cultivated, less delicate, less intelligent. He was quick to detect merit in the earlier works of rising artists; totally unbiased by the schools; and broad and generous in his applause when art-critics hesitated to commend works of real genius. With such gifts, which, had he lived, would have been developed to the honor of the State and to the credit of the Nation, our dear friend has closed his career. "Colonel Porter," says Mr. Norton, "has left a mass of half-finished manuscripts; a play incomplete; a fragment of verse; an essay here; a poem there;—if the time were not so brief between now and December, I wish they were in your hands, that you

9

might judge more accurately of his varied ability." And in a subsequent letter from this gentleman, he says: "Porter had collected all his father's papers and letters relating to the last war, with the view of writing a history of the campaign of 1812; for he was always of the opinion that such a history was a desideratum, none having been written which gave all the facts of that eventful period with the fulness and accuracy which the events demanded, and the importance of the war required."

You, Mr. President,* who can so fully estimate the meaning of this brief extract from a familiar letter; you, who have devoted your life-long labors to the history of this country upon its ancient theatre; you, who have done for the earlier actors of the colonies, and the revolution, what our beloved friend and associate intended to undertake, that we might have a true representation of the conflict which gave us the free right of the seas of all nations, as the earlier revolution gave us the free right of the lands we occupy; you, who have so laboriously built up one of the American Pyramids, can more truly than any other estimate the loss we have sustained in the younger Cephrenes.

It is, indeed, to be regretted, that so valuable an

---

* Mr. George Bancroft.

acquisition to our growing libraries should have been lost. It is true, the "correspondence, notes, and reports," of the elder Porter, may pass into other hands, and be still treasured and recorded in libraries and cabinets, as forming an extensive view of our last war with Great Britain; but, whatever may become of them, it will be a source of regret to the future student, to think that they were left without the touch of the animated pen that could have given them vitality, warmth, and coloring. In this, as in every other way, we feel that we have sustained a great public loss. Who shall fill the vacant chair, or wield the graceful pen which fled from fingers so competent?

The political life of Peter A. Porter was brief. Like his father, he was a member of the Assembly of his native State—elected in 1861. In March, 1862, he made a very spirited address to that body, in relation to a bill providing for the public defence. He, among the very few, had a true idea of the magnitude of the approaching conflict; and even anticipating foreign intervention, in which case the Niagara frontier would have been, as in 1812, the assailable point, he says: "Our frontier should be the bulwark; we should defend it. May we not hope, at all events, that the strife may be confined to our border; that, using all arms and defences that may be given us by the State and country, we shall confine *the desolation to our own farms and fields,* and not suffer the tide of blood to stain the pure waters of the Susquehanna or the rich valleys of the Genesee?"

At the outbreak of the war I had many opportunities of conversing with Colonel Porter, in relation to the aspect, civil and military, of the approaching struggle. His position in regard to it was unmistakable. Connected as he was, by birth as well as by marriage, with the Breckinridges of Kentucky; knowing, as he did, by constant intercourse with leading Southern men, much more of the policy that underlaid Southern principles than the majority of professional writers upon the subject, and being well informed, by personal observation, of the true state of the South, both in regard to its strength and its weakness, his opinions were singularly valuable, and his statements singularly clear and reliable.

But the position that he had taken was as firm as it was temperate. It was the position that became the Christian gentleman and the patriotic soldier. And in this, as in every other act of his life, he lived up to his professions. In his letter of September 5, 1863, declining the nomination of Secretary of State of New York, we find a full exposition of his views of the political aspects of the question. And even to those who do not adopt all his conclusions, the animus which pervades his political faith will be as dear to them as love of country can inspire. I do not quote this admirable letter at length, because I feel sure that it will be embraced, with many other writings from his pen, in some future volume. But I cannot avoid referring to one of his reasons for declining the nomination, namely, his immediate obligations to his regiment, the Eighth New York Artillery. "I left home," he says, "in command of a regiment composed, mainly, of the sons of friends and neighbors, committed to my care. I can hardly ask for my discharge while theirs cannot be granted; and I have a strong desire, if alive, to carry back those whom the chances of time and war shall permit to be 'present,' and to 'account' in person for all."

With this letter his political career closes. I am not aware that he gave any public expression of his sentiments afterwards; and in his military career, he was carefully "reticent" of all political matters.

In the summer of 1862, the noble infantry regiment which Colonel Porter had raised performed garrison duty in the defences of Baltimore. But to a young and inexperienced officer the position was trying and arduous. In the first place, his command was changed to a regiment of artillery. In a regiment of infantry the numerical force is, in round numbers, about one thou-

sand men, while in a regiment of heavy artillery, it is
from fifteen hundred to two thousand two hundred, men
and officers. It is impossible now to ascertain the
strength of his command, for the muster-rolls are not
open for public inspection. But from a *surmise* of the
necessary garrison of so important a post as Fort Mc-
Henry, to estimate it at two thousand men would not be
far from the truth. In the second place, his position as
commandant of one of the most important fortifications
on the Chesapeake, including, as it must have done, the
garrison of Federal Hill, assailable by land or by sea—
and, I may add, *points* that General Lee would have
struck at, had the military genius of the North failed,
either at Antietam or Gettysburg—to such a commander,
so young in military affairs, the position must have been
trying and arduous. *Arduous*, to discipline so large a
body of men, with such slight experience. *Trying*, to
feel the contingencies that might hang upon his shoulders
if he had to assume the defensive against Lee's army,
flushed with victory.

During these eventful periods of our country's history, I had a few rare opportunities of seeing him in
Baltimore and in Washington. He spent part of his
time with me in his brief visits to the capital. He was
always inquiring about our personal friends; about
"The Century," in particular, its members, its course of

action. Need I say to you how dear those conversations were? But if these were interrupted by occasional visits of army officers, just from the front, the conversation took a technical turn. Then Colonel Porter was the anxious neophyte of military knowledge. I cannot conceive of any person paying a more absorbed attention to every sentence that fell from the lips of the prominent actors of the great strife, and particularly in details, than he. What he heard then I was satisfied was carefully treasured in his memory.

Let me briefly recall here one little incident of those days. As commandant of the post at Fort McHenry, he was also the custodian of political prisoners. One day, while in Baltimore, I proposed to him to visit a friend who lived a few miles out of the city, and whose collection of pictures was well worth seeing; but Porter declined, and for these reasons: "I do not visit any persons in Baltimore," he said, "not even my own relatives. I might meet persons one day, socially, as friends, who, on the next, might be marched into the fort as captives. How could I receive as guests, and invite to my prison fare, without feelings of compunction, those who had only a short time before received me with an abundance of hospitality? Much as I would like to go, I feel that it is my duty to decline." And so, with a disposition fitted for society; with an exquisite appreciation of the fine arts; with a natural longing for something to temper the austerity of garrison life, his routine service was preferred by him, *simply because it was his duty!*

And the fine feelings of the gentleman, as well as of the officer, shine forth very clearly, when, even out of respect for some of the possible prisoners, he says, " How could I invite them to my prison fare, who had, a short time before, received me with an abundance of hospitality?" Knowing, as we now do, his feelings in regard to such matters, we can the more fully appreciate the meaning of the expression in his letter declining the nomination of Secretary of State. " We hear and talk almost nothing of politics," he says, "in our *little world.*"

And that "*little world*" of bastions and parapets, of soldiers and prisoners, bounded, for two years, a life so noble, so wise, so brave, and yet so gentle.

We can imagine, however, that there were times when he experienced a respite from the stifling boundaries of his little world: it might have been, when, in the cool of the evening, he took his accustomed walk to that famous parapet at Fort McHenry where our flag floated during the bombardment of the British fleet in 1814, the sight of which produced the immortal ode of Francis S. Key. Can we not also imagine that

73 .

those hues of our flag, which suggested the line of the poet,

"In full glory reflected, now shines on the stream"—

may have also suggested to Porter's mind the far off image of Niagara, with its national bow of promise—in full glory reflected! and that the thought might have reminded him too of that earlier war, in which his father was so gallant a participant?

I may as well recall here, too, another incident. Colonel Porter, in the early part of his military training, used to have an old sergeant, a veteran of the regular army, at his left hand, during regimental drill ; and it was his custom to consult this "*vieux moustache*" upon knotty and technical points concerning battalion tactics. Porter did not scruple to speak of this fact when talking with more experienced officers. But it sometimes happened that the sergeant was wrong. And I remember when a mooted point came up, and the advice was asked of a few military proficients, who happened to be together in Washington, that the Colonel's judgment proved to be better than the sergeant's training. And I well recollect the remark of an officer, afterwards, who had passed his life in the military service. "If your friend Porter," said he, "is not afraid to begin with a sergeant at his elbow, with what he knows theoretically, and with what

10

he will learn practically, he will become one of the most accomplished officers in the army. But," said he, "there are very few officers in the volunteer service who would dare to face their regiments with a sergeant as a tutor. It shows great firmness of character, and not a little of military shrewdness."

Colonel Porter's desire to take an active part in the field kept pace with his military acquirements. It neither preceded nor followed them. Coupled with his ardent wish for more active life, was his sense of responsibility to his regiment. He had no thoughtless impulse that would lead him to squander the lives of his men in a fruitless field, but a strong desire to carry back those whom the chances, or time, or war, should permit to be present when the result was attained and the campaign was over.

Let me now hastily refer to the movements of the Army of the Potomac which brought him into the field.

General Grant, on the fourth of May, 1864, at four o'clock in the morning, struck tents and moved upon his momentous campaign. The various battles that followed, until the left wing of the army attacked the enemy at Spottsylvania Court-House, are sufficiently familiar. But just preceding this time, such had been the heavy losses sustained in our numerous battles, that the reserve forces in garrison were called out into the field. Burnside's Corps—the reserve of forty thousand men—had been already brought to the front in the tremendous conflicts in the early part of May, of which the battle of the Wilderness was the most trying. Hancock, Warren, Sedgwick, and Meade had been hammering away with unexampled valor at the enemy's front, without gaining a permanent foothold. But the loss of men had been fearful on both sides.

At this time there were two regiments of heavy artillery commanding important points of defence on the Maryland peninsula. One was that of Colonel Porter, at Fort McHenry, overlooking the harbor and the city of Baltimore; the other was that of Colonel Lewis O. Morris, at Tenallytown, covering the approaches, on the north, to the city of Washington. These two regiments of New York Volunteer Artillery, numbering some two thousand men each, intrusted with most important positions of defence during the war, and now actively called into the field, possess, for us, a mournful interest. These regiments—the Seventh and Eighth New York Artillery —comprised the flower of the volunteer service of our State. Colonel Morris, of the Seventh, was the son of Brevet-Major Lewis N. Morris, United States Army, who was killed at the storming of the heights of Monterey, in Mexico. Colonel Porter, of the Eighth, was not less eminent in heroic lineage. Both officers entered the campaign together; both were killed on the same battle-field.

At the attack upon the defences of Spottsylvania Court-House, Colonel Porter was particularly distinguished for gallant conduct. In order to animate and encourage his men, he fearlessly rode out in the face of the hottest fire of the enemy. But the ordinary chances of battle were not the only dangers to which he was exposed. He was picked out. There was a crack of a rifle, a puff of smoke from a tree in close proximity to the gallant Colonel, as he rode to and fro. A few well directed shots from our sharpshooters tumbled a rebel out of the tree, and, upon examination, it was found that he was shot through the head. When brought in, all wounded as he was, and questioned, his Southern bravado did not desert him. "I fired," said he, "at Colonel Porter out of that tree three times, and missed him every time." The men of Porter's regiment who heard him, would have killed him upon the spot with their bayonets, but for the interposition of Porter. "Let him alone," said he. "Poor fellow, he has been punished enough. Take him to the rear." "But how did you know," said one, "that it was Colonel Porter?" "Oh, I knew him well enough," said the rebel. "I was a prisoner under him at Fort McHenry."

After Hancock's gallant attack upon Spottsylvania,

the army, by successive marches, moved over the North Anna, and crossed the Pamunkey, at Hanovertown. From "White House" it skirted the defences of Richmond, on the peninsula, and found that the open ground which had been occupied by General McClellan, in the campaign of 1862, was covered by the defences of Richmond in 1864. This may explain why it is more difficult to capture that city now than it was two years earlier.

Between the Pamunkey and James Rivers, but much nearer to the former, lies a place known as Cold Harbor. It is no *harbor*, for it is quite inland; a rolling country, not entirely cleared from the primitive forest; patches of pines and oaks are interspread here and there with Virginia farms, as well cultivated as any in that country. Cold Harbor is not a village, nor even a collection of farmers' houses; it used formerly to be a famous place for picnics and excursions from the capital of Virginia, from which it is about twelve miles distant. It has been suggested, that its shady coverts and breezy uplands gave it its original title of "Cool Arbor." But our worthy secretary* says that Cold Harbor is a common name for many places along the travelled roads in England, and that it means, simply, "Shelter without fire." The German origin of the name,

---

* Mr. Augustus R. Macdonough.

" *Herberge*," means a shelter. In this country there are now many settlements by the English formerly so named.

But, in a military point of view, Cold Harbor is a place of no little importance. Its healthy elevation above the swamps of the Chickahominy; its proximity to Richmond; to the James River on the south; the Pamunkey on the north; to the Virginia Central Railroad on the west, and the York and Richmond Railroad on the east, would suggest at once to a commander the necessity of taking possession of it. More than this, it is the centre of five turnpikes, that lead to all these important communications like the spokes of a wheel to its periphery. It is a splendid fighting country, twice famous for obstinate and determined battles. Gaines' Mill, about two miles west of it, was held for a while during the " seven days" by General McClellan; the rebels keeping possession of Cold Harbor. In General Grant's campaign, two years afterwards, and in the same month, the positions were nearly reversed—the rebels holding Gaines' Mill, while our attack was to capture the intrenchments at Cold Harbor, which would have given us the passage of the Chickahominy.

Two of the five roads that radiate from this point are crossed by another, about a mile and a half south—the two radii forming the sides of a triangle, of which the cross-road is the hypothenuse. Within this narrow

patch of earth the most deadly struggle was waged.
On the west road the enemy's rifle-pits and intrenchments covered the approach to Gaines' Mill. Early in
the morning of the third of June, orders were given to
advance against the enemy's works, and capture the
point of roads. It is necessary to say, here, that the
Seventh and Eighth New York Heavy Artillery served
as infantry in this campaign ; that these large regiments
were brigaded with what remained of several infantry
regiments, and, with these skeleton regiments, consti-
tuted the effective force of the attacking brigades. Colonel Porter's regiment was in General Gibbon's Division ; Colonel Morris, in General Barlow's ; General
Robert O. Tyler, who was chief of artillery in the Penin-
sular campaign, commanded the brigade, of which Porter's regiment formed the most effective part. To show
the numerical superiority of these artillery regiments,
let me say that one of them, with four of infantry,
would make a full brigade ; while some brigades, composed entirely of infantry, required no less than twelve
regiments. The gallant General Tyler was severely
wounded in the action, and Porter would have succeeded him in command on that field, had he lived.*

---

* General Hancock said that Porter would have been promoted for gallant
conduct, had he lived. He surely would have well won the coveted star of a
Brigadier-General, and added lustre to it.

All these commands were in the Second Army Corps of General Hancock. The mere mention of the names of these gallant officers, and of this brave corps, will recall some of the most heroic achievements of the war.

At the opening of the ball, Colonel Morris, of the Seventh New York Artillery, carried the enemy's rifle-pits, captured two hundred and sixty prisoners and several pieces of artillery; but not being supported in time was obliged to retreat, leaving his captured guns in their embrasures, but carrying off his prisoners. This was a severe blow to us. Morris had gained the key of the position at the first onset, and he had been obliged to relinquish it. To this point the rebel forces now converged in great numbers, and the fire here was as close and deadly as the opposing masses could be packed together. Against this fire Porter was ordered to advance. In response to it he made a brief address to his officers, who were summoned about him, telling them, "that it was almost certain death, but the duty must be performed." Then dismounting from his horse, he called out to his men, "Follow me, my brave boys! I will lead you!" and so, waving his sword, plunged into the terrible fire at the head of his command, and charged up to the enemy's lines. So noble and conspicuous an object could not fail to draw the fire of the rebel sharpshooters, as it had at Spottsylvania.* He fell, pierced by a bullet through his neck. Struggling to his feet, he again waved his sword, to re-encourage his charging lines. Once more he fell, this time, among other fatal wounds, struck through the heart. But with wonderful vitality, he gathered himself up on his hands and knees, and died in that position, within a few hundred feet of the enemy's works. For two days he lay under the fire of those terrible antagonists.

We lost upon and in the vicinity of that little patch of earth seven thousand men, in killed and wounded. A newspaper reporter, in describing the conflict, says, " Six hundred of the Eighth Regiment of New York Artillery lay stretched upon the field of battle."† And

---

* There was something singularly commanding and officer-like in Porter's appearance after he entered the service—a seriousness, a sense of responsibility, that impressed itself upon his fine features. His figure was moulded in Nature's best proportions; his complexion so fair that it would have been almost effeminate, had not his features possessed every mark of masculine energy. His hair was light, his eyes gray ; his face suggested a perfect type of Saxon symmetry. The broad brow, the resolute chin, the delicately curved nostril, rivalled the best specimens of classic sculpture. It is to be regretted that no cast was taken from his face. This may seem the extravagant language of a too partial friend, to everybody except to those who knew him.

† What the loss was cannot now be ascertained. An officer on General Tyler's staff, Lieutenant Pierre Van Cortlandt, in speaking of the battle of Cold Harbor, said. " I never saw such fighting. One regiment went in eighteen hundred strong, and came out with only six hundred. They went right up to the rebel works and commenced pulling out the abatis. The Colonel was killed, the Major wounded." When I asked him what regiment it was, he said, " the Eighth New York Artillery, Colonel Porter, of Niagara Falls."

these men, with all the other men from other regiments on both sides, rebel and Union, were, for the time, exposed to a cross-fire from either front. This is one of the terrible lessons of civil war!

It belongs also to the cruel history of this war to state, that Porter's own cousin, John C. Breckinridge, doubly bound to him by lineage and by marriage, commanded the rebel forces in this fearful conflict.

On the night of the second day, during a rain-storm, five men belonging to his regiment, "the sons of his friends and neighbors," whom he had promised "to account for, if alive," determined to rescue the remains of their beloved commander. They crawled as near to the enemy's works as they dare go together; then one, "holding his life in his hands," dragged himself through the mire to the body, "lying within five rods of the enemy's breastworks," tied a rope to the now useless sword-belt, and so, crawling back to the hollow where his companions were sheltered, drew him within reach of their affectionate hands. Crouching to the earth with their burden, they carried it a quarter of a mile farther, without drawing the fire of the enemy, and then placing it on a stretcher, bore it three miles through the night to the division hospital.

I am happy to be able to record the names of these gallant fellows: Sergeant Le Roy Williams had charge

of the expedition; the others were Galen S. Hicks, John
Duff, Walter Harwood, and Samuel Traviss. It would
be a grateful task for "The Century" to remember their
gallant conduct by some slight memorial. Be it greater
or less, it would not be forgotten by them.*

The body of Colonel Porter, when examined, was
found to be pierced with six bullets—two through the
neck, one through the heart, one through the abdomen,
and one through each thigh. His remains were inclosed
in a coarse coffin, made from the rough boards of a Virginia farm-house, by his faithful body-servant, John
Heany, who had been with him during the course of the
war. From Cold Harbor they were taken to White
House, Virginia, and there embalmed; from thence to
Baltimore, where they were met by a military escort, and,
with the profoundest and most respectful observances,
carried to the Episcopal church, in which he used to
attend Divine service while on duty in that city.

The rude coffin, enveloped in the dear old flag of his

---

* "The Century" has acted upon this suggestion, and appointed a committee
to prepare some suitable token, as a memorial of its affection, to be presented to
these brave men. But since this action of the Club, a new phase of the enterprise has come to light. It seems that the faithful body-servant of Colonel
Porter, who was authorized to act in such a contingency, offered a reward of one
thousand dollars to any who would rescue his remains. These five men
accomplished it, but would not accept the reward. "They would not touch it,"
said my informant. This places the action of these *braves* upon a still more
conspicuous pedestal.

country, was placed in the chancel. The funeral service was performed amid the most solemn and impressive silence. The body, after remaining all night in the chancel, was re-escorted to the cars on the following morning, and then, in the care of friendly hands, carried towards his once happy home at Niagara Falls. A large concourse from the neighboring country attended the last ceremonies that closed his brief and beautiful career. The services at St. Peter's Church were conducted by Reverend Dr. Shelton, an Episcopal clergyman, who had before performed the same sad rites over the remains of his father, his mother, and his first wife. There was no military display—no ostentatious exhibition of public processions; but the stores were quietly closed as a mark of respect, and scarcely a sound was heard in the hushed village except the solemn thunder of Niagara. After the impressive ceremonies of the Church were over, the concourse moved to Oakwood Cemetery, where the hero now rests, but not "alone in his glory."

The proposed monument is to be a simple column of marble, crowned with the emblems of his faith and his patriotism—the cross and the flag.

Fellow-members of "The Century!" in the performance of the task allotted to me I have, thus far, placed only a bare and barren record of dates and facts before you; but even the data relating to his life are so pregnant with all that is noble, wise, self-denying, indicate such keenness of perception in matters of criticism, and yet so generous in appreciation, that he was, with great gifts, so modest ; as honest in purpose as he was patriotic in principle ; and as heroic in action as he was patriotic ; and so—dying as nobly as he had lived—how can the vast storehouse of language supply epithets for a formal eulogy that will rival his simple narrative ? And can Friendship even mourn over the close of so brilliant a career, when he, in the very fulness of his chivalric nature, surrounded by a cloud of witnesses, gave up his life for his country upon that heroic field ? Is it for us to rear the commemorative obelisk or to unveil the tributary urn of tears, in memory of him whose virtues need neither pedestal nor inscription ? Let us rather turn to the more immediate relations of his blameless life, with which many of us are not so familiar.

His confidential friend and legal adviser, to whom I owe much of this brief history, says : " He was a man of the clearest perceptions in matters of business, grasping readily the most complicated affairs ; and of such sound judgment, that his conclusions were rarely incorrect." His promptness was remarkable ; he never made an appointment that he failed to keep. Once having decided any matter, he rarely found occasion to change his mind. He was exceedingly conscientious in his dealings with others. "Let us do right," he said ; "though the law gives me an advantage, I will not avail myself of it." In the hard times of 1857 he voluntarily reduced the rents of his tenants. When his mortgages were unpaid and required foreclosing, his first inquiry was, are they honest, worthy, working men? If they were, or if they had died, leaving widows or children, he always ascertained first the value of the improvements upon the property, as well as the payments they had made upon it, and generally paid the one and refunded the other." That such a course of conduct was justified by ordinary pecuniary laws we cannot admit ; but his executor says that "when his course of conduct was determined upon, he would take no other." His charities were like a rich placer, to be worked by the poor. To the friendless he was a constant benefactor. He indeed fulfilled all the injunctions of the Apostle.*

"But to all this was added yet another and higher attribute. From his earliest boyhood, his reverence for sacred things was most profound and sincere. He spoke but little of such subjects, but his whole conduct showed him to be a devoted and humble Christian." His faith was as genuine as it was unobtrusive. It guided the whole course of his spotless life. To

---

* 1st Corinthians, xiii.

those who were witnesses only of Porter's intercourse with the foam-spray of society; who merely knew him as a part of that brilliant artificial life, of which he was, upon all occasions, so conspicuous an ornament; to those this statement will appear almost incredible. But the contact of the world did not sully his pure character. Like the nobler metals, his nature could endure the fiery trial of the furnace, and run clear from the dross of the crucible. It was for many years his constant practice to acknowledge his obligations to his Creator in humble prayer, in the midst of his family, and he became a member of the Protestant Episcopal Church, in October, 1861, being confirmed at Geneva, by Bishop De Lancey. The last letter written from the front (and received after his death), contains these memorable words: "I try to think, and feel, and act as if each day were to be my last, so as not to go unprepared to God. We must hope, and pray, and believe, He will preserve me. Yet His will be done! It is selfish to wish to be spared at the expense of others."

I cannot more fitly close this brief biographical sketch of the earthly career of our dear departed friend, than by this extract from his will:

"I, Peter Augustus Porter, being of sound mind, do declare this to be my last will and testament:

feeling. to its full extent, the probability that I may not return from the path of duty on which I have entered. If it please God that it be so, I can say, with truth, that I have entered on the course of danger with no ambitious aspirations, nor with the idea that I am fitted by nature or experience to be of any important service to the Government; but in obedience to the call of duty, demanding every citizen to contribute what he could, in means, labor, or life, to sustain the Government of his country—a sacrifice made the more willingly by me when I consider how singularly benefited I have been by the institutions of the land, and that, up to this time, all the blessings of life have been showered upon me beyond what falls usually to the lot of man."

And now, fellow-members—while the accents of his departing words still linger in your ears—let me retire. I have attempted to lay a garland upon his grave, and have brought no flowers so fresh and fragrant as those that were already there. I have attempted a eulogy, and find the voice of praise is hushed by attributes above all praise. Let me dedicate, however, these few leaves to his memory, for they come from what he prized above all earthly things—the hand. and heart of a friend.

www.ingramcontent.com/pod-product-compliance
Lightning Source LLC
Chambersburg PA
CBHW020305090426
42735CB00009B/1226